THE LINDBERGH KIDNAPPING CASE, AS TOLD BY THE FBI

by the United States Department of Justice

Originally published by the United States Department of Justice, FBI Division

Republished by A. J. Cornell Publications, 2016

ISBN: 978-1541214538

CONTENTS

Overview	4
The Investigation: 1932–1934	8
Hauptmann Is Located	16
Indictment, Trial and Execution	21
Appendix: A Brief Biography of Charles Lindbergh	23

Overview

Charles Lindbergh Jr.—20-month-old son of aviator Charles Lindberg [renowned for having made the first solo nonstop transatlantic flight in 1927] and Anne Morrow Lindbergh—was kidnapped about 9:00 p.m. on March 1, 1932, from the nursery on the second floor of the Lindbergh home near Hopewell, New Jersey. The child's absence was discovered and reported to his parents, who were then at home, at approximately 10:00 p.m. by the child's nurse, Betty Gow. A search of the premises was immediately made and a ransom note demanding $50,000 was found on the nursery windowsill. After the Hopewell police were notified, the report was telephoned to the New Jersey State Police, who assumed charge of the investigation.

During the search at the kidnapping scene, traces of mud were found on the floor of the nursery. Footprints, impossible to measure, were found under the nursery window. Two sections of the ladder had been used in reaching the window; one of the two sections was split or broken where it joined the other, indicating that the ladder had broken during the ascent or descent. There were no blood stains in or about the nursery, nor were there any fingerprints.

Household and estate employees were questioned and investigated. Colonel Lindbergh asked friends to communicate with the kidnappers, and they made widespread appeals for the kidnappers to start negotiations. Various underworld characters were dealt with in attempts to contact the kidnappers, and numerous clues were advanced and exhausted.

A second ransom note was received by Colonel Lindbergh on March 6, 1932 (postmarked Brooklyn, New York, March 4), in which the ransom demand was increased to $70,000. A police conference was then called by the governor at Trenton, New Jersey, which was attended by prosecuting officials, police authorities, and government representatives. Various theories and policies of procedure were discussed. Private investigators also were employed by Colonel Lindbergh's attorney, Colonel Henry Breckenridge.

The third ransom note was received by Colonel Lindbergh's attorney on March 8, informing that an intermediary appointed by the Lindberghs would not be accepted and requesting a note in a newspaper. On the same date, Dr. John F. Condon, Bronx, New York City, a retired school principal, published in the *Bronx Home News* an offer to act as go-between and to pay an additional $1,000 ransom. The following day the fourth ransom note was received by Dr. Condon, which indicated he would be acceptable as a go-between. This was approved by Colonel Lindbergh. About March 10, 1932, Dr. Condon received $70,000 in cash as ransom, and immediately started negotiations for payment through newspaper columns, using the code name "Jafsie."

About 8:30 p.m., on March 12, after receiving an anonymous telephone call, Dr. Condon received the fifth ransom note, delivered by Joseph Perrone, a taxicab driver, who received it from an unidentified stranger. The message stated that another note would be found beneath a stone at a vacant stand, 100 feet from an outlying subway station. This note, the sixth, was found by Condon, as indicated. Following instructions therein, the doctor met an unidentified man, who called himself "John," at Woodlawn Cemetery, near 233rd Street and Jerome Avenue. They discussed payment of the ransom money. The stranger agreed to furnish a token of the child's identity. Condon was accompanied by a bodyguard, except while talking to "John." During the next few days, Dr. Condon repeated his advertisements, urging further contact and stating his willingness to pay the ransom.

A baby's sleeping suit, as a token of identity, and a seventh ransom note were received by Dr. Condon on March 16. The suit was delivered to Colonel Lindbergh and later identified. Condon continued his advertisements. The eighth ransom note was received by Condon on March 21, insisting on complete compliance and advising that the kidnapping had been planned for a year.

On March 29 Betty Gow, the Lindbergh nurse, found the infant's thumb guard, worn at the time of the kidnapping, near the entrance to the estate. The following day the ninth ransom note was received by Condon, threatening to increase the demand to $100,000 and refusing a code for use in newspaper columns. The tenth ransom note, received by Dr. Condon, on April 1, 1932, instructed him to have the money ready the following night, to which Condon replied by an ad in the press. The eleventh ransom note was delivered to Condon on April 2, 1932, by an unidentified taxi driver who said he received it from an unknown man. Dr. Condon found the twelfth ransom note under a stone in front of a greenhouse at 3225 East Tremont Avenue, Bronx, New York, as instructed in the eleventh note.

Shortly thereafter, on the same evening, by following the instructions contained in the twelfth note, Condon again met whom he believed to be "John" to reduce the demand to $50,000. This amount was handed to the stranger in exchange for a receipt and the thirteenth note, containing instructions to the effect that the kidnapped child could be found on a boat named *Nellie* near Martha's Vineyard, Massachusetts. The stranger then walked north into the park woods. The following day an unsuccessful search for the baby was made near Martha's Vineyard. The search was later repeated. Dr. Condon was positive that he would recognize "John" if he ever saw him again.

On May 12, 1932, the body of the kidnapped baby was accidentally found, partly buried, and badly decomposed, about four and a half miles southeast of the Lindbergh home, 45 feet from the highway, near Mount Rose, New Jersey, in Mercer County. The discovery was made by William Allen, an assistant on a truck driven by Orville Wilson. The head was crushed, there was a hole in the skull and some of the body members were missing. The body was positively identified and cremated at Trenton, New Jersey, on May 13, 1932. The Coroner's examination showed that the child had been dead for about two months and that death was caused by a blow on the head.

The Investigation: 1932–1934

On March 2, 1932, after a conference with the Attorney General, FBI Director J. Edgar Hoover had contacted the headquarters of the New Jersey State Police at Trenton, New Jersey. He officially informed the organization that the US Department of Justice would afford Colonel H. Norman Schwarzkopf, the Superintendent of the New Jersey State Police, the assistance and cooperation of the FBI in bringing about the apprehension of the parties responsible for the kidnapping. He advised the New Jersey State Police that they could call upon the Bureau for any facilities or resources the latter might be capable of extending. The special agent in charge of the New York City Office of the Bureau, which at that time covered the New Jersey district, was instructed accordingly and, upon instructions from the Director, the special agent in charge communicated with the New Jersey State Police and the New York City Police, offering any assistance the Bureau might be able to lend in this matter.

During the next few weeks, the Bureau was acting merely in an auxiliary capacity, there being no federal jurisdiction. However, on May 13, 1932, President Herbert Hoover directed that all governmental investigative agencies should place themselves at the disposal of the state of New Jersey and that the FBI should serve as a clearinghouse and coordinating agency for all investigations in this case conducted by federal investigative units.

On May 23, 1932, the FBI in New York City informed banks in greater New York that the Bureau was the coordinating agency for all governmental activity in the case. A close watch for ransom money was requested.

The New Jersey State Police announced on May 26, 1932, the offer of a reward not to exceed $25,000 for information resulting in the apprehension and conviction of the kidnapper or kidnappers. In compliance with a request made by Colonel Schwarzkopf, copies of this notice of reward were forwarded by the FBI to all law enforcement officials and agencies throughout the United States.

On June 10, 1932, Violet Sharpe, a waitress in the home of Mrs. Lindbergh's mother, Mrs. Dwight Morrow, who had been under investigation by the authorities, committed suicide by swallowing poison when she was about to be requestioned. However, her movements on the night of March 1, 1932, had been carefully checked and it was soon definitely ascertained that she had no connection with the abduction.

In September 1933 President Franklin D. Roosevelt stated in a meeting with Director Hoover that all work on the case be centralized in the Department of Justice. He requested the Director to convey his views to Attorney General Homer Cummings with the suggestion that the Attorney General make a request of the Commissioner of the Internal Revenue Service (IRS), either through the President or directly, for a detailed report of all work performed by the IRS Intelligence Unit. On October 19, 1933, it was officially announced that the FBI would have exclusive jurisdiction insofar as the federal government was concerned in the handling of any investigative features of the case.

The President's proclamation requiring the return to the Treasury of all gold and gold certificates was a valuable aid in the case, inasmuch as $40,000 of the ransom money had been paid in gold certificates and, at the time of the proclamation, a large portion of this money was known to be outstanding. Therefore, this phase of the investigation was emphasized.

On January 17, 1934, a circular letter was issued by the New York City Bureau Office to all banks and their branches in New York City, requesting an extremely close watch for the ransom certificates and, in February 1934, all Bureau Offices were supplied with copies of the Bureau's revised pamphlet containing the serial numbers of ransom bills. The New York City Bureau Office distributed copies of this pamphlet to each employee handling currency in banks, clearinghouses, grocery stores in certain selected communities, insurance companies, gasoline filling stations, airports, department stores, post offices, and telegraph companies.

Following the distribution of these booklets containing the serial numbers of the ransom currency, there were also prepared and similarly distributed by the Bureau currency key cards which, in convenient form, set forth the inclusive serial numbers of all of the ransom notes which had been paid. This was followed by frequent personal contacts with bank officials and with individual employees in an effort to keep alive their interest.

Prior to this time, the passing of ransom bills had been reported to either the FBI, the New Jersey State Police, or the New York City Police Department, none of which had complete information on this point. Therefore, arrangements were effected whereby investigation of all such ransom bills detected in the future could be immediately conducted jointly by representatives of the three interested agencies.

One of the byproducts of the case was a mass of misinformation received from well-meaning but uninformed, highly imaginative individuals, and a deluge of letters written by demented persons, publicity seekers, and frauds. It was essential, however, that all possible clues, regardless of the prospect of success, be carefully followed, and it was impossible in the vast majority of instances to determine at the inception whether they would be material or false.

On March 4, 1932, a con man named Gaston B. Means was approached by Mrs. Evalyn Walsh McLean, of Washington, DC, who felt that she might be of material assistance to Colonel Lindbergh in procuring the return of his child. Mrs. McLean had become acquainted with Means as a result of some investigative work that Means had performed for her husband some years before. Means informed her that he felt certain he could secure a contact with the kidnappers inasmuch as he had been invited to participate in a "big kidnapping" some weeks before but had declined. Means claimed that his friend was responsible for the Lindbergh kidnapping. The following day, Means reported to Mrs. McLean that he had made a contact with the persons who had the child. He successfully induced Mrs. McLean to hand over to him $100,000, to be used in paying the ransom, which he said had been doubled. Until April 17, 1932, he kept Mrs. McLean waiting, daily expecting the return of the child. During this period, he purported to be effecting negotiations with the alleged leader of the kidnappers, whom he called "The Fox." Mrs. McLean finally requested the return of the $100,000 and additional money that she had advanced him for "expenses." When he failed to do so, the case was turned over to the FBI. Means and "The Fox," who was found to be Norman T. Whitaker, a disbarred Washington attorney, were apprehended, and Means was later convicted of embezzlement and larceny after trust, and sentenced to serve 15 years in a federal penitentiary. Whitaker and Means were later convicted of conspiracy to defraud, and were sentenced to serve two years each in a federal penitentiary.

There were other attempted frauds, which required extensive investigations before they could be completely eliminated from consideration in connection with the Lindbergh case.

In all, there were literally thousands of leads in all sections of the United States that were followed to their definite conclusions by the Bureau. The results of all these investigations, no matter how trivial, were reported. The activities of the known and suspected members of the so-called "Purple Gang" of Detroit, and various rumors and allegations concerning this gang were carefully and thoroughly investigated. Numerous registries of boats were examined in a fruitless endeavor to locate the boat *Nellie,* on which the baby was to have been found according to the 13th and last ransom note handed to Dr. Condon at the time he paid the ransom money to "John." Records of cemetery employees who were employed in various cemeteries in certain sections of New York City and near Hopewell, New Jersey, were examined. Information accumulated in various other kidnapping and extortion cases handled by the FBI was examined in closest detail and studied with particular reference to any bearing they might have upon the solution of the Lindbergh case. Hundreds of photographs and descriptive data of known criminals of all types and other possible suspects were exhibited to the few eyewitnesses in this case in an endeavor to identify the mysterious "John."

On May 2, 1933, the Federal Reserve Bank of New York discovered 296 ten-dollar gold certificates, and one $20 gold certificate, all Lindbergh ransom notes. These bills were included among the currency received at the Federal Reserve Bank on May 1, 1933, and apparently had been made in one deposit. Immediately upon the discovery of these bills, deposit tickets at the Federal Reserve Bank for May 1, 1933, were examined. One was found bearing the name and address of "J. J. Faulkner, 537 West 149th Street," and had marked thereon "gold certificates," "$10 and $20" in the amount of $2,980. Despite extensive investigation, this depositor was never located.

Examination of the ransom notes by handwriting

experts resulted in a virtually unanimous opinion that all the notes were written by the same person and that the writer was of German nationality but had spent some time in America. Dr. Condon described "John" as Scandinavian, and believing he could identify the man, spent considerable time in viewing the numerous photographs of possible suspects and known criminals. In this connection, the FBI retained the services of an artist to prepare a portrait of "John" from descriptions furnished by Dr. Condon and Joseph Perrone, the taxicab driver who had delivered one of the ransom letters to Dr. Condon.

In a further endeavor to identify the individual who received the ransom payment, representatives of the New York City Bureau Office engaged Dr. Condon to prepare a transcript of all conversations had by him with "John" on March 12 and April 2, 1932, the dates on which Dr. Condon personally contacted the kidnapper in order to negotiate the return of the child and the payment of the ransom. These conversations were, during March 1934, transcribed in detail on phonograph records by Dr. Condon who imitated the pronunciations and dialect of "John." In this manner the nationality, education, mentality, and character of the kidnapper were more clearly defined and permanently preserved for future use.

Another interesting attempt to identify the kidnapper centered around the ladder used in the crime. Police quickly realized that it was crudely built, but built nonetheless by someone familiar with wood who was mechanically inclined. The ladder had been thoroughly examined for fingerprints and had been exhibited to builders, carpenters, and neighbors of the Lindberghs in vain. Slivers of the ladder even had been analyzed, and the types of wood used in the ladder had been identified. Perhaps a complete examination of the ladder by itself by a wood expert would yield additional clues, and in early 1933, such an expert was called in—Arthur Koehler of the Forest Service, United States Department of Agriculture.

Koehler disassembled the ladder and painstakingly identified the types of wood used and examined tool marks. He also looked at the pattern made by nail holes, for it appeared likely that some wood had been used before in indoor construction. Koehler made field trips to the Lindbergh estate and to factories to trace some of the wood. He summarized his findings in a report, and later played a critical role in the trial of the kidnapper.

Hauptmann Is Located

A series of ransom notes following the kidnapping led to a meeting between Dr. John Condon, a representative of the Lindbergh family, and a mysterious man named "John." An artist sketch of "John" was developed from the verbal description of Dr. Condon and proved to be very similar to Bruno Richard Hauptmann, who was arrested on September 19, 1934.

For a period of seven months prior to August 20, 1934, no gold certificates were discovered except for those received in the Federal Reserve Bank, previously mentioned. Starting on August 20, 1934, and extending into September, a total of 16 gold certificates were discovered, most of them in the vicinity of Yorkville and Harlem. The long-awaited opportunity had finally arrived. As each bill was recovered, a colored pin marking the location of the recovered bill was inserted in a large map of the metropolitan area, thus indicating the movements of the individual or individuals who might be passing the ransom money. When the first few made their appearance, it was decided to concentrate on gold certificates, as experience had proven the futility of tracing the ordinary currency included in the ransom money. In keeping with the cooperative policy previously established with the New Jersey State Police and the New York City Police Department, teams composed of a representative of each of these police agencies and a special agent of the Bureau were organized to personally contact all banks in Greater New York and Westchester County. As a result, the various neighborhood banks discovered the bills close to the point at which they were passed, and it then became possible for the investigators to trace the bills to the person who had originally passed them. For the first time in the history of the case, the investigators succeeded in finding that the description of the individual passing these bills fit exactly that of "John" as described by Dr.

Condon. It was determined through the investigation that the bills were being passed principally at corner produce stores.

About 1:20 p.m. on September 18, 1934, the assistant manager of the Corn Exchange Bank and Trust Company, at 125th Street and Park Avenue, New York City, telephoned the New York City Bureau Office to advise that a $10 gold certificate had been discovered a few minutes previously by one of the tellers in that bank. It was soon ascertained that this bill had been received at the bank from a gasoline station located at 127th Street and Lexington Avenue, New York City. On September 15, 1934, an alert attendant had received a bill in payment for five gallons of gasoline from a man whose description fitted closely that of the individual who had passed other bills in recent weeks. The filling station attendant, being suspicious of the $10 gold certificate, recorded on the bill the license number of the automobile driven by the purchaser. This license number was issued to Bruno Richard Hauptmann, 1279 East 222nd Street, Bronx, New York.

Hauptmann's house was closely surveilled by federal and local authorities throughout the night of September 18, 1934, until at approximately 9:00 a.m. on September 19, 1934, an individual, closely fitting the description of "John," as supplied by Dr. Condon, and the description of the purchaser of the gasoline, as supplied by the service station attendant, left his house and entered his automobile parked nearby. He was promptly taken into custody by representatives of the three interested agencies.

After some investigating, he was found to be Bruno Richard Hauptmann, the individual to whom the automobile license had been issued, a German carpenter who had been in this country for approximately 11 years. A $20 gold ransom certificate was found on his person. His description fitted perfectly that of "John" as described by Dr. Condon, and in his house was found a pair of shoes which had been purchased with a $20 ransom bill recovered on September 8, 1934. Hauptmann admitted several other purchases which had been made with ransom certificates. On the night of September 19, 1934, he was positively identified by Joseph Perrone as the individual from whom he had received the fifth ransom note to be delivered to Dr. Condon. The following day, ransom certificates in excess of $13,000 were found secreted in the garage of Hauptmann's residence. Shortly thereafter, he was identified by Dr. Condon as "John," to whom the ransom had been paid. It was also ascertained that he was in possession of a Dodge sedan automobile that answered the description of that seen in the vicinity of the Lindbergh home the day prior to the kidnapping.

A painstaking analysis of Hauptmann's handwriting by the Bureau's new crime lab showed a remarkable similarity between the lettering of the author of the ransom notes and of Hauptmann.

Shortly after his apprehension, specimens of

Hauptmann's handwriting were flown to Washington, DC, where a study was made of them in the FBI laboratory. A comparison of the writing appearing on the ransom notes with that of the specimens disclosed remarkable similarities in inconspicuous, personal characteristics and writing habits, which resulted in a positive identification by the handwriting experts of the laboratory. Upon the apprehension of Hauptmann, it was found that he bore a striking resemblance to the portrait of "John" which had previously been prepared from descriptions furnished by Dr. Condon and Joseph Perrone.

Further investigation developed that Hauptmann, 35 years old, was a native of Saxony, Germany. He had a criminal record for robbery and had spent time in prison. Early in July 1923 he stowed away aboard the SS *Hanover* at Bremen, Germany, and arrived in New York City on July 13, 1923. He was arrested and deported immediately. After another failed attempt at entry in August, Hauptman successfully entered the United States in November 1923, on board the *George Washington*. On October 10, 1925, Hauptmann married Anna Schoeffler, a New York City waitress. A son, Manfried, was born to them in 1933. During his illegal stay in New York City and until the spring of 1932, Hauptmann followed his occupation of carpenter. However, a short while after March 1, 1932, the date of the kidnapping, Hauptmann began to trade rather extensively in stocks and never worked again.

Indictment, Trial, and Execution

Hauptmann was indicted in the Supreme Court, Bronx County, New York, on charges of extortion on September 26, 1934, and on October 8, 1934, in Hunterdon County, New Jersey, he was indicted for murder. Two days later, the governor of the state of New York honored the requisition of the governor of the state of New Jersey for the surrender of Bruno Richard Hauptmann and on October 19, 1934, he was removed to the Hunterdon County Jail, Flemington, New Jersey, to await trial.

The trial of Hauptmann began on January 3, 1935, at Flemington, New Jersey, and lasted five weeks. The case against him was based on circumstantial evidence. Tool marks on the ladder matched tools owned by Hauptmann. Wood in the ladder was found to match wood used as flooring in his attic. Dr. Condon's telephone number and address were found scrawled on a doorframe inside a closet. Handwriting on the ransom notes matched samples of Hauptmann's handwriting.

On February 13, 1935, the jury returned a verdict. Hauptmann was guilty of murder in the first degree. The sentence: death. The defense appealed.

The Supreme Court of the State of New Jersey on October 9, 1935, upheld the verdict of the Lower Court. Hauptmann's appeal to the Supreme Court of the United States was denied on December 9, 1935, and he was to be electrocuted on January 17, 1936.

However, on this same day the governor of the state of New Jersey granted a 30-day reprieve and on February 17, 1936, Hauptmann was resentenced, to be electrocuted during the week of March 30, 1936. On March 30, 1936, the Pardon Court of the State of New Jersey denied Hauptmann's petition for clemency, and on April 3, 1936, at 8:47 p.m., Bruno Richard Hauptmann was electrocuted.

APPENDIX

A BRIEF BIOGRAPHY OF CHARLES LINDBERGH
by Charley Rodriguez

Charles Augustus Lindbergh was born in Detroit, Michigan, on February 4, 1902. When he was two months old, the Lindbergh family moved to a farm at Little Falls, Minnesota. Although the farm was his real home, Charles lived in many places while he was growing up. Starting in 1907, he spent winters in Washington, DC, with his father, who was a congressman. His summers were spent in Little Falls on the farm or traveling with his mother. When he was eight, his parents started him in second grade at Force School in Washington. His mother had tutored him up to his age level. This was the first of eleven different schools he attended in a ten-year period. Charles was not particularly interested in school subjects. He liked more active things, such as farming, shooting guns, and anything that had to do with mechanics. Charles graduated from Little Falls High School in 1918 at the age of sixteen. In 1920 he entered the University of Wisconsin. While a student at the University, he joined the Army ROTC program, served on the ROTC rifle team, and attended artillery school.

Charles Lindbergh's greatest desire was to learn to fly. In April 1922 he enrolled in a flying school at Lincoln, Nebraska, but was never given the opportunity to solo. Instead, he went on tour with a barnstorming act where he learned to "wing walk" and to perform as a parachutist. A year later, he went to Americus, Georgia, and bought a surplus "Jenny" training plane for $500. After one 30-minute flight with an instructor pilot, he soloed. He remained at Americus for a week developing his ability to control the plane. Then he departed on a very long, circuitous, barnstorming route for Minnesota.

In 1924 Charles Lindbergh passed the Army entrance exams and entered training as a flying cadet at Brooks Field, Texas. In March 1925 he graduated number one from his advanced training class, but he did not receive a regular commission, so he returned to civilian life. Lindbergh traveled the country as a barnstormer until he took a job as an airmail pilot. He spent a year flying mail between St. Louis and Chicago.

In September 1926 Charles Lindbergh decided that he would make a solo flight across the Atlantic. He got the necessary financial backing and contracted with Ryan Airlines to build the special airplane he would need. The airplane was ready for test flights by the end of April 1927. At 7:52 a.m. on May 20, he took off from Roosevelt Field, Long Island, New York, in the *Spirit of St. Louis* and landed in Paris, France, slightly more than 33½ hours later. He received a tremendous welcome in Paris and upon his return to the United States. As a result of this flight, he was promoted to the rank of colonel in the Army

Reserve. Also, he received a prize of $25,000 for being the first person to make a nonstop solo flight across the Atlantic.

In July of 1927, Lindbergh, in the *Spirit of St. Louis*, went on a goodwill tour of the country. The purpose of this tour was to promote commercial aviation by showing people that an airplane could get from city to city quickly and on a precise schedule. The tour lasted slightly over three months and covered 22,350 miles. His next pioneering flight took place in December of 1927. He took off from Washington, DC, on the 13th and landed in Mexico City the next day at 3:00 p.m. It was during this trip that he spent Christmas with American Ambassador Dwight Whitney Morrow and his family. It was at this time that he met Anne Morrow, who would later become his wife. He left Mexico City on the 28th and flew the *Spirit* on a tour that included thirteen Latin American nations. Everywhere he went he was greeted by enthusiastic celebrations. In 1928 Lindbergh went to work for two airlines, Transcontinental Air Transport and Pan American Airways. His job with both airlines was to promote air travel and to establish air routes. On May 27, 1929, he married Anne Morrow. The following year their first child, Charles Lindbergh Jr., was born. In 1931, flying a new Lockheed, custom-built airplane, Lindbergh and Anne, an accomplished aviator in her own right, embarked on a polar flight to the Orient to chart a polar route for Pan American Airways. Beginning on July 9 and ending on December 19, 1933, Charles and

Anne undertook survey flights for Pan American Airways to determine which of three possible transatlantic routes was the best. It was during this time and in 1932 that tragedy struck the young Lindberghs. Their young son was kidnapped and murdered.

In 1934 President Franklin D. Roosevelt decided that the Army should take over flying the mail. Charles objected and made public statements warning of crashes and deaths that would follow such a course of action. His predictions proved true and Roosevelt was politically embarrassed. From that time on he disliked Lindbergh. By 1936, the Lindberghs could no longer tolerate the curiosity seekers and newsmen who constantly interrupted their privacy, so they moved to England. From there, Charles and Anne visited Germany, France, and Russia. He was received as a "world hero" but in reality, he was busy gathering information on the capabilities of these countries for aerial warfare. He passed all of this information to Washington.

Charles and Anne Lindbergh moved back to the United States in 1939. Almost immediately, Colonel Lindbergh began speaking out against U.S. involvement in a war in Europe. He believed America was not militarily prepared and that its civilization might be destroyed. Because of statements and accusations that were made against him by President Roosevelt and others, Colonel Lindbergh resigned his Army commission. When the Japanese attacked Pearl Harbor in December 1941, the question of U.S. involvement in war was settled. Charles Lindbergh now wanted his commission reinstated so he could do his part in the war. President Roosevelt would not permit this unless Charles publicly admitted that he had been wrong. He could not do this because he still believed he had been right, so he found other ways to help his country. For the remainder of the war, he served as a civilian consultant to the Ford Motor Company and to the United Aircraft Corporation. With United Aircraft Corporation he flew fifty combat missions during a tour of duty in the Pacific. In 1954 President Dwight D. Eisenhower and the U.S. Senate returned Charles Lindbergh to the Air Force Reserve as a Brigadier General.

After the war, Lindbergh became involved in a number of tasks, some of them for the Air Force, others for commercial aviation, and others for personal and business interests he had.

By this time, the Lindbergh family had grown to three boys and two girls. So, they settled in their country place in Darien, Connecticut. Later they moved to a smaller house in Darien and began dividing their time between Darien, Switzerland, and Hawaii. Busy though their lives were, Charles and Anne always had time for their children and grandchildren.

When doctors in New York told Charles he was dying, he immediately left for Maui, Hawaii, to spend his last days. He died August 26, 1974, and was buried on Maui in the Hawaiian Islands.

Made in United States
Orlando, FL
26 December 2024

56546931R00017